How To Ove Childhood Trauma The Easy Way

Step-By-Step Guide on How to Overcome a Rough Childhood to Chart a New Path in Your Life Free from Childhood Baggage

Introduction

A child is born clueless about the world, defenseless and helpless. They can only depend on their caregivers, parents, or guardians to inform them, protect, care for, and guide them.

So, you make a grand entrance into the world. You don't even know to expect good things and a good life; you simply are a child. At this point, the people into whose lives you enter have full responsibility to give you the life they think you deserve. We should hope that every child gets the best and is given a head start to help them flourish. This is so for some.

So, what happens when you come into the world clueless, and the people you have known, the ones you automatically trusted to keep you safe the moment you opened your eyes, become the very people that hurt you? What if the people supposed to protect you become the ones you ought to fear and run from?

Like every other child, I was born into a family that, by societal norms, was supposed to love and protect me. Unfortunately, I feel into the hands of a man who thought I was fit to be used for his sexual pleasures at the age of five. You may expect that man to have been a mean stranger. But no, that man was my father.

I remember he would creep into my room at night when my mom fell asleep. I remember every time he touched my almost invisible nipples and my thighs. I really don't know how he found a 5-year-old girl attractive sexually. Maybe the fear and terror in my innocent eyes gave him a hard-on.

I did not know right from wrong. I did not know what my father was doing was wrong. I just knew that the pain I felt was excruciating when he did it. I only asked myself why he did not stop when I cried and why he would put his hand over my nose and mouth until I could barely breathe when I screamed in pain. Did my daddy not feel bad for me when I cried? Didn't he care that he was hurting me? And why did he tell me not to tell anyone?

I was too naïve, and I often wondered whether my friend's fathers did the same thing to them. Little did I know, I was a victim of sexual abuse by the very man who sired me. There was nothing okay with what he was doing. I was too innocent; I just didn't know. I did not know how to say no to him, report him, or do anything to save myself. Do you know what's worse? My mother knew about it.

She had actually walked in on him molesting me many times. What did she do? Nothing! She watched her little girl crying in pain, all bloody and bruised, and did nothing. Actually, she would punish me if I went to talk to her about it.

So, you can understand when I tell you that I grew up looking at rape as normal. My father would hit me when I tried to resist, and I learned to let him have his way. He would choke me when I screamed, so I learned to let the tears flow without making a peep.

By the time I was twelve years old, I was living my life like his sex slave or puppet. By this time, I had learned that it was not right for a father to do this to a child. I knew it was not normal, and I was an abuse victim. What bewildered me then was that my mom could see everything that was going on and the fact that I was losing my mind and my innocence at the same time and did nothing to stop her husband. My mother neglected me, and my father hurt me. I never knew what tenderness or love was.

"Well," you might think, "why I did not ask for help now that I was older." The truth is, I wanted to, and I tried. I was ashamed to talk about what was happening to me, mostly because my parents made it seem like I was at fault for some reason. I thought that anyone else would judge and condemn me.

What's more, when I mastered the courage to try and seek help, my father always found out about it and trashed my claims. He said I was a rebellious kid looking for attention. At home, the sexual attacks became worse. He would rape me six times a day, and my cries seemed not to bother both my parents. The only solution I had was to train myself to accept violent behavior. I felt dirty and unworthy. I was withdrawn and did not have friends. My world was collapsing on my little head, and I had nowhere and no one to run to. I felt trapped!

When I was old enough to get into relationships, my dad was still a hovering shadow. Normal teenagers have dates and can introduce a boyfriend to their families. That was not the case for me. My father couldn't stand to see me with another man. Soon enough, no boy wanted to associate with me because my dad had built a reputation of giving hell to any of my love interests. You would think he was being protective of his beloved daughter. But no, he was jealous and protective of his decade-long sexual slave.

It was too much for me, and I decided to run away. I had been looking for a way out of that life. At that time, running away felt like the best way to get away from all the evil and put whatever had happened to me behind me. I was going to start on a clean slate and have a wonderful life from there on. And for the first time, I felt alive, like a renewed human being.

I had never known love in my life. I was anxious to give it – and mostly to receive it back. I thought that this would somehow rid me of the feelings of emptiness and heal my soul. My universe was centered on finding someone to love me. I did find them, but it was turned out not to be what I expected.

I went from one relationship to another, but no one seemed capable of giving me what I was looking for. In fact, most of the people I fell in love with turned out to be abusive, callous, and selfish, just like my father. It was like his ghost was following me everywhere I went.

The very past that I was running from was following me everywhere. I didn't understand why the faster and the further I ran, the quicker it caught up with me. I thought I was cursed and doomed to suffer. I called myself unlucky, and I hated myself and hated my life.

Why couldn't I ever get the things I desired?

Why was I not having any good experiences?

Why did I fall for abuse after abuse? Why did I not have the good relationships I worked so hard to create?

I never understood why my past was following me until after I got help. I wasn't unlucky. I had trauma from the terrible experiences in my childhood. The memories of the incidences and the emotions from that period had buried themselves into my subconscious. They influenced every decision and choice I made.

That is why I subconsciously fell for abusive men and tried hard to fix them. This was because back then, I encountered such a man in my dad and I had desperately wanted him to be better.

So now, I believed someone abusive could be better – and I assigned myself the job of making them better. Yes, I was falling for broken men; their brokenness attracted me, and I would play healer and get hurt in the process. It was a vicious cycle. I didn't know why I would always repeatedly make such choices, go through unimaginable pain, and still do the same thing again. Therapy saved my life, and now, I am successfully turning over a new lease of life.

Were you abused as a child?

Anyone who was abused as a child is more likely to get abused as an adult. This is according to an analysis released on 27th September 2017.[1]

Like me, you may have had a rough childhood in one way or another, and due to the stigmatization and ridicule that

---

[1] https://www.ons.gov.uk/peoplepopulationandcommunity/crimeandjustice/adhocs/007527impactofchildabuseonlaterlifecrimesurveyforenglandandwalesyearendingmarch2016

surrounds this topic, you have not talked about the trauma or sought help. You could have tried everything within your power to put your past behind, to change your story, and have a good life, but nothing has changed.

I was once where you are now, but through therapy and a journey to inner self-healing, I've learned a lot that has helped me overcome that trauma. I wrote this book for people who have been where I have been and want to overcome and flourish in life.

This book contains everything I have done so far to heal and live a better life. If you asked me how many times I tried to move on as an adult and succeeded, I would write another whole book. You see, as adults who have gone through mistreatment as children, we always think that we have everything under control; we always think we are strongest. The truth is, we are weak, and we need immediate help.

I used to ask myself questions like:

- Why can't I stop thinking of those people who hurt me?

- Will I ever stop feeling this pain?

- How can I get over the fear of being abused?

- How will I ever forgive those who caused me pain?

- Will I ever have a better life?

- Will I ever stop suffering?

- Will I ever find someone who will love me for who I am?

- How can I love again?

If you relate to these questions, this book will answer them in a language that you will understand and guide you towards a better life experience.

This is what you will learn from this self-help book:

- Facts about childhood trauma.

- Childhood trauma prevalence and the types involved.

- Impacts of childhood trauma in adulthood.

- How to heal from childhood trauma.

And much more!

This book might open old wounds, but allow it to walk with you through a journey that will lead you to a new path in your life free from childhood baggage!

PS: I'd like your feedback. If you are happy with this book, please leave a review on Amazon.

Please leave a review for this book on Amazon by visiting the page below:

https://amzn.to/2VMR5qr

Table of Contents

Introduction ___ 2

Chapter 1: Childhood Trauma (Scope of the Problem) ___ 13

Chapter 2: Childhood Trauma: How Much Do We Know? ___ 18

    Child Abuse ___ 19

    Trauma from the child's environment ___ 22

    Child neglect ___ 24

Chapter 3: Effects of Childhood Trauma ___ 26

    Childhood Trauma's Impact On Shame, Guilt, And Stability ___ 27

Chapter 4: The Road To Recovery: How To Overcome Childhood Trauma ___ 34

    1. Acceptance: Recognize and acknowledge the trauma ___ 35

    2. Unburdening Through Forgiveness ___ 42

3. Moving Away From Your Role As A Victim 49

5 Steps to Get Free From the Chains of Victimhood _____ 52

4. Practice Self-compassion _____ 60

How to Practice Self-Compassion For Healing 63

5. Take Care Of Yourself _____ 66

What is self-care _____ 67

How to practice self-care _____ 68

Conclusion_____77

Chapter 1: Childhood Trauma (Scope of the Problem)

I know how it feels when you have been hurt and have gone through more pain than anyone could understand. You feel different, and sometimes you look at yourself like a weirdo.

I know how it breaks the heart when you look at others, see that they look okay, and you think that you are an outcast because you are the only broken one. I know how lonely this path can get when you feel alone, or as if you are the only one on this path and that no one can understand where you are coming from. But you are not alone.

The first step towards overcoming childhood trauma is to accept yourself as you are right now and stop feeling like an outcast. Some so many people have been there. Don't look around and when you see smiling faces, assume that everyone but you is happy and has had a beautiful life experience. You are not alone, and you are not a weirdo; many have, are, and will continue walking down the healing journey you're on right now.

If you look at the following statistics detailing the prevalence of child abuse in our communities, you will believe me when I tell you that you are not walking this journey alone.

General statistics show that 7.9 million child abuse reports have been recorded. CDC has broken down the general number of children being abused to one in every seven children[2]. From all the fatalities recorded, around 70.3 percent of the abuse cases were caused by at least one parent[3]. The World Health Organization has also revealed that three in four children aged two to four suffered various forms of child abuse at the hands of their parents and caregivers[4].

Going into specific statistics, American SPCC reports that from 7.9 million children, 491,710 are neglected, 115,100 are physically abused, 60,927 are sexually abused, 39,824 are psychologically maltreated, and 29 states report 877 victims being sex trafficked[5]. Another body, the National Children's Alliance, reports that 678,000 children were victims of neglect and abuse in 2018 alone[6]

Deaths are also considered when child abuse is mentioned. American SPCC states that 45.5 percent under one year die because of child abuse. Of all recorded deaths caused by child

---

[2] https://www.cdc.gov/violenceprevention/childabuseandneglect/fastfact.html
[3] https://americanspcc.org/child-abuse-statistics/
[4] https://www.who.int/en/news-room/fact-sheets/detail/child-maltreatment
[5] https://americanspcc.org/child-abuse-statistics/
[6] https://www.nationalchildrensalliance.org/media-room/national-statistics-on-child-abuse/

abuse, only 50 to 60 percent are recorded[7]. Childwelfare.org, through data they got from the National Child Abuse and Neglect Data System, we get to know that 51 states reported 1,809 fatalities. The same organization tells more – 72.9 percent of deaths were caused by neglect or by a combination of neglect and other forms of mistreatment[8].

The really sad thing about child abuse and neglect is that most adults have a hard time coming out and sharing how they were abused as children. This means there could be more hidden cases within our society, and the situation could be worse than is currently presented.

The World Health Organization, for example, indicates that only 5 women and one in thirteen men have mastered enough confidence to report that they had been abused as children[9]. This means that only one-quarter of all adults report being victims of abuse as children.

This is worrisome because it means the extent of the problem is not certain and that many people are walking around with trauma buried deep and influencing how they see and react to the world.

---

[7] https://americanspcc.org/child-abuse-statistics/
[8] https://www.childwelfare.gov/pubpdfs/fatality.pdf
[9] https://www.who.int/en/news-room/fact-sheets/detail/child-maltreatment

One of the key things about trauma is that if you have not gotten to the point of putting it out in the open and getting help, it stays in your subconscious mind, controlling how you think, feel, and whatever you do.

This could be why we have a lot of people suffering from anxiety and stress disorders, others turning into psychopaths, people hurting others, and a lack of empathy and compassion in our society. This is why we have many people who are "people" on the outside, but inside, they are shattered, which manifests in their actions.

American SPCC also notes that from all the convicts in prisons, 14 percent of men and 26 percent of women are reported to have been abused as children, which is twice the number seen for those who are not in prisons[10] which shows the extent of abuse in our society.

From these statistics, you can see how child abuse is rampant and how if nothing is done, things only get worse. It may be assumed that the abused child will 'get over it' as they grow, but we can see that adulthood is not an escape. The trauma of that experience is likely to follow an individual for life.

---

[10] https://americanspcc.org/child-abuse-statistics/

If you are having a hard time moving past what happened to you, I want to encourage you:

Even though the journey to recovery may be painful and challenging, it is a journey well-worth taking and that you can get through. If you want to have a better life, this is what you have to go through. It is, therefore, important that you believe in yourself and have faith in the process. Keep going when things get hard, and stay committed. I promise you, when you cross over to the other side where your trauma doesn't control you, you will realize that everything you put into this was worth your while.

Akshay Dubey said that healing does not mean the damage never existed. It means that the damage no longer controls our lives." Your goal is not to let the past control and dictate what you do now.

Let us look at the different types of childhood trauma next; that way, you'll be better placed to recognize what you are dealing with:

Chapter 2: Childhood Trauma: How Much Do We Know?

Based on the National Institute of Mental Health, (NIMH) childhood trauma is:

"The experience of an event by a child that is emotionally painful or distressful, which often results in lasting mental and physical effects."

On the other hand, The National Child Traumatic Stress Network[11] states that whenever a child feels "intensely threatened by an event he or she is involved in or witnesses," then this is trauma.

Kindly note that the different types of trauma we will discuss fall under what is known as the Adverse Childhood Experiences (ACEs). This term originated from a study done in 1995 by the Centers for Disease Control with the help of California's Kaiser Permanente Health Care Organization[12].

This study categorizes childhood trauma into three main categories and ten sub-categories. Kindly note that these are

---

[11] https://www.nctsn.org/what-is-child-trauma/about-child-trauma
[12] https://www.cdc.gov/violenceprevention/aces/index.html

not the only ones, rather, they are just a part of them and the most common. They include:

Child Abuse

Physical abuse

The result of this abuse causes physical injury to the child. Simply put, this abuse causes non-accidental physical injury to the child.

Despite the legal definitions of this abuse varying from state to state, the physical injuries are all the same. They may include, red marks, bruises, cuts, welts, broken bones, or/and muscle sprains.

Under physical abuse, we can break it into;

Sexual abuse

Any sexual contact between an adult and a child is considered sexual abuse. The abuse can be;

- *Touching or kissing; that is, the adult doing the touching with an intention of sexually arousing the child.*

- *Fondling the genitals or the body parts in a prolonged manner or in a sexual manner.*

- *Oral-genital contact or any manual stimulation of genitals or intercourse.*

Sexual abuse can also be defined as any behavior aimed at arousing a child or any behavior intended to stimulate the offender using the child. This includes showing the child any erotic materials, taking sexually explicit photographs of the child, or using any sexually-induced talk with the child.

Sexual abuse could also be defined as sexual contact by anyone who is older than the child. Despite these definitions varying from state to state, they always refer to the same thing.

Emotional abuse

If your parent or caregiver made you feel 'good-for-nothing,' alone or scared, then you were emotionally abused. For you to understand this type of abuse better, you can call it psychological or verbal abuse. This abuse includes;

- *Being criticized, humiliated, or/and blamed*
- *Being isolated*
- *Being ignored or rejected*
- *Being made different from others*

- *Being forced to meet unrealistic or unreasonable expectations.*

- *Being treated unfairly due to things you could not change, like a disability and/or gender.*

- *Being blackmailed to do something. For example, you might have been forced to pose naked or have your pet killed.*

- *Being exposed to domestic violence.*

Emotional Neglect

If you lacked any response to your emotional needs, then you were probably emotionally neglected. Your parents might have provided all necessities for you but failed to consider and meet your emotional needs.. For example, Peter often told his parents that he was always sad because of another child at school. However, Peter's parents always brushed it off as foolish childhood games. Over time, Peter learned that his emotional needs were simply childish and therefore stopped seeking for any support no matter how sad he got. This is a good example of being emotionally neglected.

Trauma from the child's environment

Parental substance abuse

If your parent(s) or caregiver(s) were either physically, emotionally, or sexually abusive because of their long history of drug and/substance abuse, then this is considered as parental abuse.

Parental separation and/or divorce

If you experienced behavioral and/or emotional problems as a child after or during your parent's divorce or separation, then you can consider this as part of childhood trauma.

The thing is, it is rare for separation and/or divorce to go smoothly and because of all the back and forth and the verbal and physical wars that happened, you might be experiencing lots of failures as an adult ranging from failed relationships to behavioral disorders.

Mentally ill or suicidal families

Growing up with a family member who suffers from mental illnesses is not easy. At school, if this news got to other students, you might have gone through ridicule, shame, and guilt. At home, you might have gone through physical, emotional, and/or emotional abuse from the caregivers of the patient. Remember that if your parent or guardian was mentally ill and he/she hurt you in one way or other, then we will not title that as abuse because it was not deliberate.

Violence to parent

Just like Shania Twain, who witnessed her mother being abused by her father, you might have gone through the same. This is a form of childhood trauma that affects a lot of adults. Watching one of your parents being tortured does not leave and despite many knowing it, the complications you might be having for example with relationships might have been as a cause of what you went through as a child.

Imprisoned household member

This form of trauma cuts in deep. Losing one or both parents or guardians to the justice system creates a lot of problems in the family. For example, financial problems will tend to arise because all the responsibilities were left to one parent or guardian, missing a mother or a father figure in the house may have made you emotionally neglected.

Child neglect

Physical neglect

This type of neglect is by far the most common. To note if you went through neglect, your parent or caregiver failed to provide the basic needs like clothing, shelter, and/or food. Simply put, you were left without supervision for an extended period of time.

Educational neglect

If your parent kept you from doing things or attending things that could have changed your life for the better, then you were emotionally neglected. For example, if you were barred from going to school and the same parent or caregiver refused to go for homeschooling as a substitute.

Emotional neglect

Some parents who deliberately ignore, reject, threaten, and/or isolate their children. These parents and caregivers successfully create an environment of fear by denying the child the social interaction, attention, and support that they need to grow. If this is the kind of childhood you went through, then unfortunately, you were neglected.

Medical neglect

Were your parents in a position to offer you with all the basic needs you needed including access to healthcare but when you got ill, they deliberately refused to take you to receive such care? This is a form of neglect which can be considered as abuse. There are cases where the children in question get so ill but because they cannot receive the much needed healthcare, child services need to be called in so as to help alleviate the situation.

As we have seen in this chapter, there are several types of child traumas. This past cannot be changed – what happened then cannot be altered because the hand of time cannot be turned back. Many of the powerhouse names I have used as examples in this chapter knew one main thing; their past could not be changed or forgotten, edited, or erased. All they could do is accept it since they believed that their future was in their power.

In the next part of this book, we begin the permanent healing process. We will first look at the impacts of what you went through as a child and how the same manifests itself right now as an adult. Knowing these impacts will help pave way for you to get to the most important part of this book; ways of overcoming your rough childhood so that you can finally chart a new path in your life free from childhood baggage.

Chapter 3: Effects of Childhood Trauma

Signe Hjelen, Jan H, Bente Traen[13], and Per-Einar were on a quest to find out how adult women who had gone through childhood trauma were fairing on in their quest to move on from their past. The thirty-one participants who took part in the research, and with the help of the findings recorded after thirteen interviews were done showed that the ladies believed that;

- *Finding new ways to understand their actions and emotions,*

- *Finding ways to move from the numbness they felt towards other people,*

- *Finding ways of becoming self-advocates of their own needs,*

- *Finding ways to feel wanted and,*

- *Finding ways of living without the difficult feelings brought about by the childhood trauma was the only way to get better.*

---

[13] https://www.ncbi.nlm.nih.gov/pmc/articles/PMC3892724/

As an intervention, I believe that it is vital for us to find out what prompted these participants to settle for these strategies and the only way to do so is to get into their shoes and assess the damage that was done.

The thing is childhood trauma affects adults in several ways:

Childhood Trauma's Impact On Shame, Guilt, And Stability

Without any doubt, the trauma you went through has proved to have immense power over your life. It has robbed you off your childhood, has made you loose your grip on important aspects of your life which has caused you nothing but instability in all spheres of your life, and has made you undermine yourself since everything and everyone seems to be against you. All these limitations have damaged you to a point all you feel is shame and/or guilt and trying to rise above and beyond your trauma only to fall down again brings in nothing but irritability, anxiousness, and depression.

For me being abused by a close person in my inner circle as a child impacted all my relationships as I grew up and by the time I was an adult, I had little to no connection with others. I started seeing those who wished to be close to me as predators. Basically, I could no longer trust anyone who said he/she cared and loved me because my sense of identity was long fractured and building it took longer than I had initially thought.

Childhood trauma leads to adult attachment disorders

Now that you are an adult, you may have tried to live a happy life; you may have desired to start a family, fall in love with that guy or lady you have had a crush on for months or years, or get into a partnership with someone but you simply cannot and it might be draining all happiness from you. The reason for your failure to move on permanently is because all the physiological state memories, the motor vestibular memories, and the emotional memories you had as a child were stored in your brain and now as an adult, going through something similar, may it be true or false, triggers all those emotions which manifests themselves as fear of interpersonal attachment or mistrust.

Toby Ingham, a UKCP registered psychotherapist and a member of the training committee of The Guild of Psychotherapists and The Association of Psychotherapists[14] says that,

---

[14] https://tobyingham.com/about-me/

"If you come from a background with good attachments, you are more likely to develop good attachment as adults"

Simply put, being neglected by your parents for example has affected the way you relate with your family because you simply do not know how to bond in that way. The bond you went through as a child was disorganized which makes you approach all attachments with some fear of abuse and neglect since its all you know.

Having attachment disorders as an adult normally does not occur alone. They are linked with disorders such as:

- *Alexithymia.*

This disorder comes from lacking emotional awareness. Simply put, this disorder makes you have challenges identifying and describing your feelings. You will also have difficulties in distinguishing bodily sensations that arise from emotional arousal. A study done to examine the link between somatization, childhood trauma and alexithymia found that physical abuse and emotional abuse and neglect can cause this disorder[15].

15
https://www.sciencedirect.com/science/article/abs/pii/S016503271200496X

- ***Avoidant-dismissive insecure attachment***

This disorder is closely likened to alexithymia. While alexithymia will make you have a challenge when distinguishing emotions, avoidant-dismissive insecure attachment will make you avoid any form of intimacy or any sort of closeness.

- ***Depression and anxiety***

You might be the kind of person who internalizes emotions as a coping mechanism and in as much as it seems to be helpful, the downside of this strategy is that it makes you vulnerable to developing additional psychiatric problems. A study was done to examine the link of childhood trauma and depression in chronically depressed patients. The results of this study was intended to shed more light on the relationship between trauma type and depression. Using 349 participants for the study, the researchers found that childhood trauma led to more severe depressive options[16].

Closely associated with depression is parental functioning. From the hard relationship that I had with my parents, it took a lot, which I will share in this book, to help me be in a place where I could cultivate a healthy bond with my

---

[16] https://www.ncbi.nlm.nih.gov/pmc/articles/PMC4677006/

children. The thing is, there are many factors that will make parenting difficult because this is an art you lacked as you grew up.

- ***Addiction***

You might be wondering why you cannot break your addiction. The thing is, if your parent was an addict, then you are at a huge risk of being an addict too. As an adult, the attachment disorders you have might be as a result of your parents' addictions. Researchers in Libya decided to carry out a study to assess the relationship between attachment styles and addictions. The results they gathered showed that the adolescents who had insecure attachment disorders had high chances of being cigarette, alcohol, and waterpipe addicts and if no monitoring could be done to manage the situation, the said adolescents would develop future substance use disorders[17].

The stress involved in trying to move away from what happened to you as a child might have turned you to alcoholism. Michael, Kaitlin, Katarina, and Fred did a study that discovered that their findings *"were consistent with a development model where dysfunctional parental bonding*

---

[17] https://bmcpsychology.biomedcentral.com/articles/10.1186/s40359-020-00404-6

in childhood manifests in adulthood as insecure attachment and alexithymia...[18]"

- **Eating disorders**

For example, the link between sexual abuse and eating disorders has been documented as noted by Eggleston Youth Centers, Inc[19]. This does not mean that only sex abuse is behind eating disorders. Emotional abuse, for example, is known to lead to low self-esteem, issues surrounding body image, and self-critique. This means that unhealthy eating habits, which often result in eating disorders, become a mechanism used to maintain control whenever a person feels overwhelmed.

Glenn Waller, Emma Corstorphine, and Victoria Mountford sought out to find the link between emotional abuse and eating disorders. From the results of the study, the researchers noted that the going through emotional abuse as a child will make it hard for you to develop better emotional skills that are important in bonding with people. The lack of a healthy emotional background also may cause alexithymia, caused poor distress tolerance, and will make it hard for you

---

[18] https://onlinelibrary.wiley.com/doi/full/10.1002/jclp.22772
[19] https://www.egglestonyouthcenter.org/blog/the-link-between-childhood-trauma-and-eating-disorders/

to inhibit emotions[20]. Simply put, these two statistics shows that childhood traumas can alter with your quest to get healthy and fit.

---

[20] https://bit.ly/3kX00kz

Chapter 4: The Road To Recovery: How To Overcome Childhood Trauma

As mentioned earlier, the journey towards freedom from childhood traumas is quite challenging, not to mention long. It may require a walk down memory lane, to that darkness and those painful experiences, which can bring them to life. However, as hard and as painful as this journey may be, it is one you need to take if you are ready to set yourself free from that darkness that has been controlling you.

This process will require you to remain committed and persistent when things get hard and patient because trauma that took years to cement in your mind will not suddenly heal overnight.

As you get started on the journey to inner healing, remember that it is okay if the path gets uncomfortable and sometimes difficult and painful. When it does, press on and do not give up; stay committed and trust the process, even when it doesn't seem like it's working, and even when you don't feel like doing it anymore.

The small actions you take daily to overcome childhood trauma will eventually compound and move you closer to healing and better living. Isn't this worth your while? It is.

Let's get started;

1. Acceptance: Recognize and acknowledge the trauma

Years after experiencing childhood abuse, how have you been looking at that abusive period in your life? My way of coping was to look at it like it wasn't that bad. Other times I would just tell myself that it didn't happen. Also, there were times when I just pushed those thoughts to the back of my mind and occupied myself with other things.

According to experts, many victims of childhood trauma spend years minimizing or dismissing the event as a coping mechanism; others succumb to feelings of guilt and self-blame. Others come up with excuses to justify the event or the perpetrator's actions. Psychological trauma experts believe that we do this because explaining what happened gives us comfort and may seem to make the load lighter.

For instance, excuses like 'they were young' 'they were high on drugs and didn't know what they were doing" "they were helpless addicts," "they were going through a lot of pain themselves," and so on – just to make it seem like what they did to you was a helpless reaction on their part.

You could have been using these mechanisms to cope with those terrible memories and insecurities arising from what happened to you, sometimes unconsciously. But this doesn't make them go away, does it?

Acceptance marks the beginning of healing

There is no way to heal from something you pretend you are not suffering from. When you close off your heart and mind to the reality of what happened to you and your current life experience because of it, you will struggle to heal.

That is why the first step towards healing from childhood trauma is to acknowledge that wound in your soul, accept that it is a part of you. What happened to you is not a bad dream or an imagination in your head. It happened, it was bad and painful, and, in one way or the other, it has contributed to making you the person you are today. Acceptance is your starting point in this journey.

It can be tough to come to terms with this kind of reality. I know how hard it is to finally stop running and turn back and face these ugly things you have run from all your life. It is scary and hard, and I know it takes a lot to do this, but I also know that you are strong enough to do this. Start believing in yourself as much as I believe in you as you take the following three steps that will help you start accepting any childhood trauma:

Step 1: Self-knowledge

All acceptance begins with self-knowledge: knowing yourself at a deeper level. Fortunately, self-knowledge is not all that hard to achieve if you're willing to take some action:

- *Know how you feel*: It is important to know your emotions, how you are feeling right now, and how you feel when you go back to the memories of the past. The emotions may not be pleasant.

  For instance, you may feel anger or fear when you think about your past, and right now, you may be feeling overwhelmed, uncertain, fearful, etc. These emotions arise within you for a reason; start accepting that they exist and approach with compassion and understanding. Don't label any of them as negative. Allow yourself to feel them and sit with them.

- *Know your body*; You may need a moment here to sit in a quiet place and allow yourself to be physically present in your body, to notice every sensation. Notice how your body feels, from your toes to your crown. For instance, do you feel a tightness in your chest, heaviness in your mind, or an uncomfortable feeling in your stomach? This helps you know and understand what's going on in your body and also figure out why.[21]

Now connect your emotions to your body sensations – because there is always a connection between how you are feeling and how your body feels. For instance, fear may trigger a strange tightness or uneasiness in your stomach, while anger may show up as a tightness in your chest or head, etc.

Now ask yourself, do I know why I am feeling this way? Go through the events in your day or week. Is there anything that happened that relates to these feelings? Does your past experience or any relation to them have something to do with how you feel right now?

For instance, maybe someone you love betrayed you, and you went back to how a loved one betrayed you in the past. As a child, you believed that you were abused because you were

---

[21] Understanding, Supreme, et al. *Knowledge of Self*. Supreme Design Publishing, 2009.

not worthy of love. This memory causes you to make their betrayal about yourself and who you are instead of who they are and their choices. You start to blame yourself, which makes you feel angry and helpless and physically manifests as being tired, stressed, head or chest pain or heaviness, etc.

This shows how self-awareness can help you understand yourself, your feelings and reactions, and where they come from. It allows you to no longer be under the automatic control of the unconscious mind. When you are self-aware, you are awake to what is happening within, you can see the truth of a situation, and you have the power to influence and control how you perceive and feel about things – and how you react.

The essence of self-awareness in trauma healing is to help ensure you know who you are and recognize and accept the things that made you the way you are; it is about being awake to how you feel in mind, body, and soul, and understanding why you feel so.

This is about getting comfortable with spending time with yourself and that trauma every day, getting to know her and the effects she has in your mind and body and the person she's made out of you.

It is an uphill task and quite uncomfortable, but if you can do this, it means you are ready to rewrite your story. Despite what happened to you, you are taking responsibility to make yourself the person you want to be and create the experiences you want to have in life.

Step 2: See things for what they really are

When we go through challenging times, we tend to invest a lot of time and energy into twisting the reality to see things for what we want them to be. We get carried away by our imaginations and lose touch with our reality. This avoidance is a common coping tactic, especially if you have had unpleasant experiences that you hate to look back on.

To see things for what they really are is a significant part of acceptance. If you want to accept the past and how it has shaped your future, you need to tame your imagination and train yourself to start looking at things as they are.

Success tip: Differentiate between acceptance and preference

We often fight off acceptance because it feels like we are surrendering to the things that have hurt us – the things we want to get as far away from as possible. Ignoring reality makes us feel like we have regained some power and somehow succeeded.

However, this is a false sense of victory. This delusion leaves us weak and vulnerable to even greater injury because sooner or later, our truths will catch up with us, and we will be too weak to deal with it.

Accepting something is not the same as preferring it or even supporting it. Consider the following illustration; [22]

You are having fun at the beach, swimming with your friends, and the water starts to pull you too far from the mainland. The current gets too strong for you, and you can barely fight to stay afloat. What can you do?

To save your life, even if people know you to be a great swimmer, you must first accept that you are no longer in control and are drowning. Does accepting that you are drowning mean surrendering to the water and letting it take you out?

No, it means you are awakening your mind and senses to the dangerous situation you are in so you can intentionally do something to rescue yourself. Now, imagine if you want to pretend that the water is just playing with you or that you are still in control. You will certainly drown, won't you? It works the same way for your childhood abuse and trauma.

---

[22] Bernard, Michael E. *The Strength of Self-Acceptance*. Springer Science & Business Media, 2014.

Accepting that it happened, that you feel bad about it, and that it has negatively influenced your life does not mean you are surrendering. You are simply in a space where you are looking at things as they are and allowing them to be, without imagining that you have a responsibility to change or control how it might have been or should be.

Other than accepting that someone did bad things to you, you also need to accept that there is still a hurting and traumatized child trapped inside you. Accept that you have often used their viewpoint to look at the world and interpret your experiences. But most importantly, it's time to quit feeling sorry for yourself or blaming your abusers.

What happened is in the past and can't be changed. Fortunately, the present and future are in your hands. Accept that now you have a responsibility to take charge of your life, heal that inner child, and set yourself free from this trauma to be healthy in mind and soul and create the beautiful life you deserve.

2. Unburdening Through Forgiveness

Forgiveness is a crucial part of the healing process. After acceptance, this is the second way you make peace with your past and heal yourself.

What comes to mind when you hear the word forgiveness, especially regarding the people that caused you so much pain?

I remember this step took me quite some time because I could not imagine that I was being asked to pardon people who caused me so much pain. They were adults and I was the child! They knew what they were doing to me; they were supposed to protect and to love me, but they chose to violate me. It was as if they enjoyed to see me in pain and they ruined my life. How was I ever going to forgive that?

I could not imagine it. When my therapist brought up the question of forgiveness, it would be the need of that session because I would get so mad and emotional that we couldn't work through anything. I was confused and had so many questions.

Was she siding with my enemy? Why was she telling me that I ought to forgive when she knew exactly what they had done to me? From where I stood, my parents deserved all the anger, resentment and hate that I felt towards them. Forgiveness would never be something they would get from me.

But I did change my mind about it? Yes, I did, when I was educated about the importance of forgiveness in healing. I found that if I was going to warm up to forgiveness for all that had happened, I was doing it for me; for my sanity and my own well-being. This was less about them and more about me.

If you are struggling to embrace forgiveness, read on and find out why this part of the journey is essential for the resolution of that trauma, and why you should take this high road for your sake.

What is the meaning of forgiveness in trauma healing?

Many have used the word forgiveness all their lives, but a good number does not know what forgiveness really is. It is assumed that forgiveness means reconciliation, dropping grudges and coming together with people who hurt or wronged us, to continue living as if nothing happened. That is what they mean when they say 'forgive and forget' right?

Thinking about what you were put through, it is understandable if you cringe to the idea of forgiveness in these terms. You are right to reject the idea of 'forgive and forget'. I know firsthand, that it cannot work, especially in regards to people who have experienced horrific traumas at the hands of other people.

Therefore, we are not going to view forgiveness from the same perspective as an ordinary person. This is not about pardoning those who hurt us; this is about dealing with the pain and the trauma made worse by the feeling of anger and resentment towards what happened to us and our perpetrators. We are going to call this un-burdening, in other words letting go.[23]

The process of unburdening

This is about letting go of those chronic feelings of anger, resentment, bitterness and hatred. Yes, you have a right to hold all these in; just do it if you don't intent to ever feel better. You see, these are negative and unhealthy emotions that do not contribute towards healing and will not help exacerbate the trauma.

If you choose to keep them, for example you choose to stay angry at your abusers and have a mind of vengeance, whose mind and soul will these emotions be polluting? Yours alone. The other person may be going on with their lives oblivious of the storms in your mind.

---

[23] lford, C. Fred. *Trauma and Forgiveness*. Cambridge University Press, 2014.

You will find that you won't be able to do anything positive to help move your life forward. You can't even focus on your work, finding new opportunities, self-development and things like this which will make your life better. These emotions will drown your hope and dim your light. This is why holding on to these emotions is more like ingesting poison and expecting the other person to die.

By making the choice to release these emotions, you do yourself a great favor; You rid yourself of toxic baggage.

How do I forgive, and how will it help in healing trauma?

As we have discussed, forgiveness is about you unburdening yourself and not about them getting pardoned. This is not to suggest that you forget what happened to you or what they did. This is to ask you to set yourself free from it all. There is no way you can hold the anger without holding on to the trauma. If one stays, they all stay.

So, now that I forgive, how am I supposed to feel when I think of that past or when I think of them? You may ask. Well, you are allowed to feel what you want to feel. What you should not do is dwell on those negative feelings any longer. Accept, acknowledge the thoughts and emotions as they rise and let them flow freely without stopping to attach to them or make sense of them. Do not even try to suppress them. You should just let them be.

When you are no longer dwelling, they will eventually lose their grip on you. Meanwhile, you will be intentionally adding on what you want to feel and experience. You will invite positive thoughts, keep your mind busy with positive action for self-development and healing and fill your soul with hope. This will create a light that if allowed to shine long enough, the darkness will have no choice but to give way to.[24]

Forgiveness invites light where there has been darkness. It takes the toxic baggage off your back and sets you free. When you let go of the negative emotions, you leave space in your heart and mind for positivity.

This excerpt from **'Anger Management Sourcebook'**, by Schiraldi and Kerr will help you understand what forgiveness means for trauma and how it helps. [25]

Forgiving means that we choose to release resentment, hatred, bitterness, desires for revenge for wrongs done to us; it is a way to come to peace with the past. In forgiving,

---

[24] Ransley, Cynthia, and Terri Spy. *Forgiveness and the Healing Process.* Routledge, 2004
[25] Anger Management Sourcebook, by Schiraldi and Kerr

we decide to break our troubling connection to the offender. We realize that no offense is worth the price of destroying our peace.

Forgiving is taking the arrows out of our gut, rather than twisting them around inside us. We move away from it beyond the offender and the offense and take full responsibility for our present happiness. We choose to forgive so that we will suffer less and be free to live.

Forgiving is a personal choice that does not depend on the offender's deserving it, asking for it, or expressing remorse– although this certainly can make forgiving easier. Forgiving is about the offended person's inner strength, rather than the offenders. We voluntarily forgive because we realize that getting even does not heal." [p. 182]

Note: Forgiveness after trauma is a life-long journey and a pathway that unfolds. It will not be done overnight. Allow yourself to mourn and to be angry. Cry and wail if you have to. But whatever you do, let it be a release; no dwelling or holding on.

3. Moving Away From Your Role As A Victim

When terrible things such as abuse happen to us, it is not easy to let go of the pain and forget what happened to us. This is only natural, and there is nothing wrong with it because you were hurt and such is unforgettable.

However, this is not the reason many people have a hard time breaking away from the traumas of the past. Most of us cannot beat trauma because we slipped into the role of the victim and adopted a victim mentality which makes us a victim of our circumstances.

In this headspace, you wallow in self-pity; you feel sorry for yourself. You feel like the world is against you and like you carry its weight on your shoulders. You feel unfortunate and disadvantaged. This keeps you weighed down and stuck. It sucks up your strength and willpower and at the end of the day little to no action is taken to get unstuck or make your life any better.

You will find that what hurt you years ago is still keeping you pinned on the ground, unable to move. It is still taking from you and making you miserable, and because you are in the victim role, you believe that you have no power to move past it.

Drop the tag

Yes, you were a victim of abuse, that's a fact. This has not only been a memory, but it has been a tag on your forehead that you have carried all your life. It is engraved into your subconscious mind and has been influencing your life unconsciously.

You stepped into the role of victim, rightfully so because this is what you were. But this is not who you are now, and this is probably not who you want to be for the rest of your life. Let me tell you why;

In the role of a victim, you remain as powerless as when you were in those dark days. It means that you still have the control and power of the offending person in your life, still hurting and tormenting you. [26]

Victimhood will not make you any better, no matter how many years you put on those shoes. It will keep you tied to your past and the pain from it. I did it for many years, and

---

[26] Wiest, Jeannine. *The Alchemy of Self Healing.* Red Wheel/Weiser, 2014

perhaps you have too. It didn't improve me or change the fact that I was abused. It just made me weaker by the day.

Stepping away from this role helped break the shackles of pain and suffering from my past. This helped me turn over a new lease of life. It made me feel stronger and much more in control of my life and my future. I owned up to the fact that I couldn't change the past but, in my hands, I had the power and time to create the life I wanted now and in the future. I understood that the longer I stayed feeling unfortunate, the longer I was delaying my healing and progress. So, I stepped out of that role, for the sake of my life and my future.

When you step away from the role of the victim, you shed all the dark influence of the perpetrators, to step into and own the power and light that you possess. You release yourself from the prison of 'unfortunate me' 'poor me' and you put an end to your suffering. This helps heal your trauma.

5 Steps to Get Free From the Chains of Victimhood

Acknowledge your emotions about the harm that was done to you and work to release them.[27]

Shift your mentality from victim to survivor

"I am a survivor" is an acknowledgment that bad things happened to you, while at the same time acknowledging your power and ability to overcome and rise above it. "I am a victim" is also an acknowledgment that something bad happened to you but it is an admission of weakness and resignation to fate, circumstances and trauma to do whatever they want to you.[28]

Say these words out loud. Which one makes you feel strong? For me, it is "I am a survivor."

---

[27] Recognize and Overcome Victim Mentality. CreateSpace Independent Pub, 2012.

[28] Siebert, Al. *Survivor Personality*. Penguin, 2010.

In the book ***"What Doesn't Kill You Makes You Stronger,"*** Maxine Schnall says this about these two mentalities;

- A victim asks how long it takes to feel good – a survivor decides to feel good even when things are not so great

- A victim would seek retribution – a survivor would seek redemption

- A victim grinds into a halt – a survivor keeps putting one foot in-front of the other

- A victim argues with life – a survivor embraces it

What can we establish from her words? It is clear that a victim mentality will only serve to make you feel worse, to wish that you could change a past (which is impossible) to make you feel powerless and keep you stuck. This mentality will have you hating your life and doing nothing to change it. It says "Yes, I was abused and my is so terrible because of it. I will probably never be happy or free from this trauma. I am doomed."

On the other hand, a survivor's mentality will encourage you to keep moving forward in understanding that you cannot change the past. It tells you not to hate or wish away your life but to embrace it and take the initiative to create the life experience that you desire. It says "yes, I was abused, but I am not letting that be the story of the rest my life. I survived and I believe I will thrive."

Choose and adopt the survivor mentality.

Build self-confidence

Abuse tramples on your self-esteem as abusers tend to make you feel like you are a lesser and un-worthy being. It takes away your confidence and you may walk through life feeling and acting like a lesser being, and being sort of comfortable with it – by taking on the role of a victim.

Generally, confidence helps you feel better about yourself and to cultivate a positive 'I can' attitude and mentality. [29]

A confident person believes in themselves and they feel powerful and in control. They have that go-getter attitude, to believe they can get what they want if they put their mind to

---

[29] Leedham, Andrew. Unstoppable Self Confidence: How to Create the Indestructible, Natural Confidence of the 1% Who Achieve Their Goals, Create Success on Demand and L. 2019.

it. This means that there is no room for self-pity or 'oh poor me' attitude.

Feeling confident again will make you feel strong again, to believe in your abilities to improve on whatever you are struggling with and give back your sense of worth – to believe you are valuable and worthy. This will help you break away from victimhood

The good thing about confidence is that it can be taught or built and improved upon in any person.

Practice gratitude

Bad things have happened to you, but you are still here. You are reading this book today because you are blessed and favored. This is something to be grateful for, don't you think?

Just think about it; there are people out there who just lost their sight, others lost their lives and others are going through trauma and they haven't had the opportunity to read such a book – a book that gives them hope. Also, there are those who have had their whole lives completely wrecked by these traumas and they don't even know it – they think they are unlucky or cursed.

But you know its trauma, you are breathing and you can read this book. Yes, you are blessed and that right there is a reason to be grateful. I bet you that these are not the only blessings you have. Look around you with intention to find something good in your life. There will be plenty.

So, if you are this blessed, why would you let yourself wallow is self-pity or feel like a helpless victim?

A wiseman once said, "people see what they look for and hear what they listen for." This means, if you are intentional about finding something to hurt for or complain about, you will find it. Likewise, if you are intentional about finding your blessings and things to be grateful for, there will be plenty. If you want to heal and break the shackles of victimhood, do the latter.

When you can see and become a witness for your blessings, then you will create a positive mindset and less will be the times you go back to thinking 'poor me.' This is you stepping out of the role of victim, and into your power. [30]

---

[30] Cruise, Portia. The Healing Power of Gratitude. 2019.

Take responsibility for your life

Someone hurt you in the past and you were their victim, there at their mercy. If you managed to escape that situation, you are no longer at their mercy, but yours. Right now, in this moment, you have a responsibility to yourself to move from the place where they left you and fight for the life that you want.

Yes, you were hurt. But unless you move to heal and better your life, you may forever remain the way they left you. Trauma doesn't heal by itself; you have to take measures to help yourself heal. If you have been sabotaging yourself because of that trauma, you have to become aware of these tendencies and become intentional about entertaining thoughts that support you.

I would like to tell you that someone will be so good to do it for you, but I will be lying. There may be people who love you and they will assist and support you. A therapist will be there to guide. But you, only you can make the healing happen.

Knowing that your life is your responsibility and so is the life you want to create, and taking this responsibility seriously will help you come out of the victim role. What's more it will empower you to believe that you can heal and create the life you want. [31]

Perform acts of courage

This will be where you take steps of faith, step out of the victim comfort zone and do things that you would usually shy away from – things that would set you free and make your life better.

For instance, say you have been afraid to say 'no' because you don't want to be rejected. You agree to it and later feel helpless as you deal with the consequences thinking 'I had no choice.' This is submitting to victimhood, because you truly had a choice.

The next time someone wants you to do something you don't want to; you are going to feel your mind going into that

---

[31] Smith, James F. Own It! How to Take Responsibility for Your Life - Step Up to the Mirror. 2013.

victim space because it is used to. Be intentional about pulling it from that side and into courage and say no.

The first time is going to feel a little awkward and you will be really scared of those consequences you have dreading – of people leaving you. Just do it, as long as you know it is the right thing to do for you. Do this again and again until you get comfortable with it.

You will find that your fears were not as scary as thy seemed. For instance, you may be rejected and people may walk away from you. but how much unwanted situations will you have avoided? How much better will you feel when you stand by your principles and do the things that actually want to do?

Soon enough, their approval may not matter as much as it did and your world will not end because they left. It will feel better to be at peace with yourself and get left than to be with people while at war with yourself.

This is just but an example of an act of courage. Examine yourself and your experiences and take steps that you have believed impossible, steps that will make your life better and heal you.

Take the bold steps of action. Believe you can and just do it! This is the most practical way to step away from the role of a victim. It's going to be uncomfortable at first, but it will feel so great on the other side, you won't want to go back.

4. Practice Self-compassion

"Self-compassion is the ability to notice our own suffering and to be moved by it, making us want to actively do something to alleviate our own suffering," offers Kristen Neiff, one of the world's leading experts on self-compassion.

Self-compassion basically stands for "kindness directed towards self". It is about self-love and self-care which is crucial for trauma recovery.

The pain of unresolved trauma from childhood often presents itself as self-critical thoughts, feeling intolerant to our imperfectness, mistakes and struggles or engaging in self-harming behaviors such as condemning ourselves or even inflicting physical harm. [32]

It affects a person's ability to be kind to themselves such that when you look in the mirror, you don't see yourself through loving eyes as you would someone you love. All you can see is

---

[32] eff, Kristin. *Fierce Self-Compassion.* HarperCollins, 2021.

the damage, the scars, the pain and the anger and the unfortunate events turning up in your life as a result of the trauma. You see yourself as a faulty human being and often you will exclaim "what is wrong with me!"

For example, I had so much difficulty maintaining relationships because of the childhood trauma that I still carried around with me. I should have extended compassion to myself when a relationship with an abusive partner ended. But do you know what I did? I would fault myself. I would look in the mirror and say "you are a terrible person, that's why no one loves you. That's why he mistreated you and could stay with you." Talking to myself like this only intensified my trauma and worsened the relationship I had with myself. I saw nothing good in me, and I hated myself and my life.

Needless to say, things only got worse because of this. When you don't have a good relationship with yourself, you cannot have it with others. What's more, you cannot see any talents or abilities in you and you won't be able to set any goals or have any ideas in your head. This is because there is such a self-loathing tornado always swirling in your head that there is no peace or space for any positive thing to happen. This means that it will be impossible to develop or improve yourself and every new day becomes yet another opportunity to inflict more suffering on yourself.

Just like abuse from others, self-hostility affects our ability to manage stress and can lead to mental health problems such as depression. A great relationship with ourselves is paramount to our wellbeing, mentally, emotionally and even physically.

Such a relationship can be made when we practice self-compassion. It allows us to soften our hearts and mind, to see the good and to see what can be done to change things – or to accept what cannot be changed. It is the beginning of experiencing ourselves as worthy beings – worthy of kindness, forgiveness and all good things.

How to Practice Self-Compassion For Healing[33]

Keep that inner dialogue positive

There is always an inner dialogue going on in our minds, whether we are conscious of it or not. It offers commentary and gives opinions about everything that we experience and even our thoughts. This conversation has a tremendous effect on how we see and feel about ourselves.

The trouble with this dialogue is that it often leans on the negative. If we are not conscious of it an intentional about making it positive, it will say ugly things, lead us to self-loathing and self-sabotage.

For instance, you are in a party and you notice someone attractive. The first thought that comes to mind could be "you should go over and talk to them." Before you can move, the inner commentator comes on to tell you "Look at yourself.

---

[33] How to Be Nice to Yourself - the Everyday Guide to Self Compassion. Althea Press, 2019.

Such a person would never be interested to speak to someone like you."

Entertain this conversation long enough and you will hear about how unworthy you are, and there will be proof of how certain people have treated you in the past to prove it. You will end up feeling so much worse about yourself and probably walk the rest of the party feeling unconfident and unworthy, not talking to anyone.

This will always happen to you whether in a party, a boardroom or in your room by yourself if you don't become conscious and manage your internal dialogue.

Watch how to talk to and about yourself to yourself. Differentiate between the voice of your fear and trauma, and the voice of your true self. Those negative things are coming from a dark place in your subconsciousness. For every negative thing they say, counter it with positivity. If it says, you are not worthy, say "I am worthy and valuable".

Accept and love yourself for who you are

Most of us have ideas about who we 'should be' which makes us not appreciate or accept who we really are. To be self-compassionate is to accept yourself for who you are – all your flaws, imperfections, the nice stuff, everything!

You are beautiful and special, just the way you are - and you were made like that for a reason. Tap into the power of your special qualities, your strengths and your gifts. Accept your weaknesses and the things that are not so good about you as a part of you. Maybe you would like to be better. But growth starts from acceptance.

Thinking about what we 'should be' may trigger negativity and self-loathing, feelings of unworthiness and not being 'enough' which will not help in healing your already wounded soul and self-esteem.

I know you may not like everything about you. Self-acceptance is not about loving everything there is about ourselves. It's about acknowledging and accepting ourselves for who we are.

Have a fair attitude towards yourself

Self-compassion entails treating yourself gently, warmly, and fairly as you would a person you love. Its about having an attitude of acceptance and understanding rather than a critical or judgmental one. It is about being kind to yourself.

Reflect on your self-talk and how you treat yourself. Does it feel like something you would be okay with saying to your most beloved person? Talk to yourself as you would someone you love. Think about that person that you love; it could be your friend or your child etc. How do you speak to them? I bet you do not tell the hurtful things. Treat yourself and talk to you as you would to them.

Understand that it is okay to struggle

Healing and being normal does not mean that you will not struggle – with emotions, with work, relationships and life in general. Understand that struggle is a normal part of life, and many times it serves the purpose of stretching us and teaching us valuable lessons.

To struggle does not indicate weakness or inefficiency. It does not mean that there is something wrong with you. This is something we all experience as human beings. Use your struggle not to condemn yourself but to learn. Ask yourself "what is this trying to teach me?"

5. Take Care Of Yourself

Having trauma means that you do have some wounds from the past; wounds that need to be nursed so they can heal. And its not just the past, every-day life with its struggles and consistent stressors will often hurt us – and the pain will be much worse if you have pre-existing wounds from your past.

This is why self-care is very important not only for healing but also for your well-being hence forth. [34]

What is self-care

This can be defined by the term itself; basically, it is taking care of yourself. It is a multifaceted process of engaging in strategies that promote our health and enhance well-being.

Everything that you do with the intention to preserve or enhance your physical, emotional, spiritual or mental health is regarded as self-care. It helps in building resilience towards life stressors – some of which you cannot eliminate.

For instance, stress and anxiety is inevitable in life, for anyone. If you cannot cope well with it, there will be a negative impact on your mental health. However, if you have a self-care routine that involves meditation, then you have a tool to unburden and take care of your mind so that it can thrive in spite of the stress.

---

[34] Care, Self, and Ankita. Self-Care: A Course in Self-Care: Heal Your Body, Mind & Soul Through Self-Love and Mindfulness. Self Care, Self Love, Self Com, 2019.

How to practice self-care

There are five types of self-care; Physical, social, mental, spiritual and emotional self-care. Below are examples of things that you can do to practice to practice each type of self-care on a daily basis;

Mental self-care

Did you know that the way you think and the things that you fill your mind with can greatly affect your psychological well-being? A great part of mental self-care is being intentional about the things that you give your mental space and energy to. This is especially important in trauma management and recovery, because as they say, "its all in the mind".

Mental self-care activities

This involves activities that keep you mentally healthy such as;

- Meditation and mindfulness – this help manage the mind chatter and keep us grounded in the present moment. Learning to live in the present will be of great help in helping to stop ruminations about a painful past (that cannot be changed) and focus on the present that we do have the power to influence and create better experiences.

- Intentional positive input – we can make our minds positive by managing the things we feed into them. For instance, by watching shows, documentaries, reading literature or listening to audiobooks that support the kind of life experience we would like to have. This will help change the narrative in our minds and change our perspective about life.

- Engage in cognitive development activities that enhance your creativity and sharpen your focus. For instance, learning a new skill, enrolling for classes to pursue something you have always wanted to do, reading books, takin an art or creative class to learn drawing, dancing, singing etc.

These activities will help you grow and improve yourself, while keeping your mind focused on constructive things. It will improve your focus, empower you with new ideas and some of these activities are also meant to relax your mind and give you a positive vibe.

Emotional self-care

We may not be able to avoid the unhealthy emotions that we may experience at times. However, having healthy coping skills to dela with these emotions will help us stay emotionally balanced and healthy.

One may think that avoiding negative emotions is self-care but to the contrary, this is self-damaging. Emotions are best not suppressed – as they may create more stress and problems for us when not addressed.

Practicing emotional self-care

Emotional self-care includes activities that help us acknowledge, accept, process and express our emotions in a healthy way, for instance;

- Sharing with someone about how you feel – this person can be a therapist or a loved one you can trust who listens and validates your feelings without judgement. This helps you to unburden yourself emotional and express yourself. Sometimes, speaking out your emotions will help put these feelings into perspective, to understand why you are feeling that way – and you can find solutions that help you feel better. Other times just talking about it will make you feel lighter and better.

- Engaging in leisure activities that help you process your emotions. For instance, if you love walking, taking a walk say near water or any other natural environment can help make you feel unburdened.

- Other emotional self-care activities involve journaling, working out, listening to soothing music, doing something that makes you happy for example if you love trying out new recipes, drawing, going out shopping etc. On healthy ways of expressing emotion, learning how to be assertive and self-control should help curb unhealthy emotional reactions.

Physical self-care

We may take this to be about fitness but there is more to benefit from physical self-care than having that perfect body. There is a strong connection between your body, mind and soul. When you are caring for your body and are physically healthy, you will find that you will think and feel better too.

To practice physical care, consider the following;

- How you are fueling your body; what are you eating? Healthy eating habits and nutritional foods are crucial for physical wellness.

- How much sleep are you getting? Sleep will have a huge effect on how you feel emotionally, mentally and physically. If you have been sleep-deprived, you know how hard it can be to focus and also how cranky and tired you feel. This is why you should get enough sleep; at least -8 hours of sleep.

- How much physical activity are you doing? Exercise will not only get you physically fit but it will also help lift your mood and reduce stress and anxiety. Establish an exercise routine that you can be consistent with. It can be as easy as taking a 30-minute walk or jogging around your block in the morning.

- Are you taking care of your physical needs? Your body will always tell you what it needs. For instance, if you need a break from work, your body will communicate through fatigue. If you need water, you will feel thirsty. If you feel unwell, you need medical care. Listen to your body and catering to your needs will help you fix a lot of problems before they can grow.

Social self-care

We are naturally social beings. To our kind, the human kind, interacting with others is a necessity. The state of our social lives and our relationships can either make or break us. Keep in mind that social health requires not just interactions for the sake of it but healthy interactions and relationships with others.

How to practice social self-care

- Develop close connections with like-minded and healthy individuals. For this to happen, you will need to put in the time and energy into building healthy relationships.

- Create social boundaries; learn to say no to others, even if they are your best-friend, when you need to say yes to yourself. These boundaries will ensure that you take care of yourself and your needs even when you are socially active. They will eliminate the need to avoid people because we feel that they are 'too much'.

Knowing where others stop, what you can or cannot take from others, is a healthy way of making sure that relationships never get toxic and you can enjoy a healthy social life.

- Stay around or connect with people who care about you and make you happy. Have fun, have a laugh and engage in activities that you both enjoy.

Spiritual self-care

Nurture your spirit. This has nothing to do with religion. Rather, it involves things that help you connect with your inner self, develop a deeper sense of meaning, understanding and connection to the universe, and to connect you with a divine power higher than yourself.

How does this help, you may ask? There will be times when you cannot make sense of life, the world or what's happening around you. There will be days when your strength alone will not be enough to get you by.

A strong connection with your inner spiritual self will help you make sense of things, by giving you an understanding deeper than what you can see and feel in the physical world. When things get messed up here, you can go higher to find your peace. You can always seek divine intervention and divine healing by leaning on that divine power higher than yourself. This means you will always have somewhere to run to, and a greater power to lean on.

How to practice spiritual self-care

- Find your purpose and engage in activities that align to it.

- Connect to a higher spiritual authority through prayer, meditation etc.

- Connect to your inner guide; your intuition which is regarded as the voice of the inner being, and learn to take its counsel.

- Engage in activities that enhance your connection with inner self such as yoga, meditation, reflection or a spiritual support councilor or group.[35]

Note: Get professional help

You may need to seek professional guidance to help you walk through the trauma journey and get your healing. This is a person who is experienced in dealing with situations like yours and they are best suited to help you navigate the path.

---

[35] Media, Adams. *The Little Book of Self-Care*. Simon and Schuster, 2017.

It would help you to have someone experienced, and someone who is not experiencing all the emotional and mental challenges of this journey hold your hand steady as you navigate these waters.

It is okay to seek professional help. Do not be ashamed that you have to, regardless of what anyone may say. This is for your Healing. Do this for you.

Conclusion

Trauma is as a result of past pain or suffering will live in your subconscious mind and continue to wreak havoc in your life. Do not allow something that happened to you, and people who hurt you to continue defining your life.

It is not easy, but it is possible to unburden yourself off the past and live a new healthy life free from that trauma. You can decide to do that for yourself today.

PS: I'd like your feedback. If you are happy with this book, please leave a review on Amazon.

Please leave a review for this book on Amazon by visiting the page below:

https://amzn.to/2VMR5qr

Printed in Great Britain
by Amazon